Writing: the team at Normandie Junior (Jean-Benoît Durand, Nathalie Lescaille and Estelle Vidard).
Art direction: Gaëlle Queval – Layout: Jean-François Gehenne.
Illustrations: Laurent Lolmède, Sandrine Lemoult (mascot).
Cover: Jean-François Gehenne / Detail from the Bayeux Tapestry, 11th century.
With special authorization from the town of Bayeux.

Translation: Chrystelle Lerouilly.

2008, Normandie Junior Éditions
www.normandie-junior.com
47, place du Général-de-Gaulle
76000 Rouen

ISBN 978-2-916538-15-0

Act 49-956 of July 16th, 1949 relating to publications for young people.

Printed in France by Kapp, Évreux (27).
Copyright 1st published June 2008.

William the Conqueror

Normandie junior
ÉDITIONS

Contents

William the Conqueror

To go further

Chapter 1

William's childhood

Does the name William the Conqueror ring a bell? Before he became Duke of Normandy and King of England, this famous knight had an eventful childhood! Here is the beginning of his adventure...

It's a boy!

William is born at the end of the year 1027 in Falaise, Calvados. He is the son of Herleva, the daughter of a local merchant and Robert, Duke of Normandy. Herleva is not Robert's wife, William is an illegitimate child. He is to be called "the Bastard". Yet, Robert wants him to be his heir as he is his only son.

J.-P.Nivet/Town of Falaise.

The Falaise castle where William was born still exists. You can visit it.

Help!

In 1035 William is 8 years old. His father decides to go on a pilgrimage* but before he leaves Normandy, he tells the Norman lords that William is to succeed him when he is grown up. The lords want to seize the opportunity to take over the Norman duchy. They attack William's kinsmen. In a few months' time, the duchy is put to fire and the sword. William has to run away!

* Words in colour are explained on page 24.

Franck Dion/Town of Falaise.

At the age of 15, William is « dubbed ». He becomes a knight during a ceremony.

When he finishes learning his trade, the knight-to-be is generally between 18 and 21 years old. The dubbing is a major step in his life! During the ceremony, he vows he will be good, loyal, generous, he will fight in the service of the church and he will defend the weakest. In exchange, he receives a sword blessed by the priest. He is a knight now! When he dies, his eldest son will inherit his lands and will be able to serve the same lord.

Learn+

What is the feudal system?

In the Middle Ages, knights are warriors from noble families. They fight for a more powerful lord or the King. In exchange, they receive land and other benefits. Here is how it works!

The overlords

are high-ranking knights. From their castles they reign, in the name of the King, on large lands protected by their army. For example Duke William reigns over the Duchy of Normandy.

The feudal society

is like a pyramid with the King at the top. Each lord is a vassal to a more powerful lord: the overlord. A man can thus be the vassal to one lord and a lord to several vassals all at once. For overlords like William, the one at the top is the King! At the homage ceremony, the vassal pledges obedience and loyalty to his lord.

The vassal

receives land, the fief, and benefits from the lord's protection (or the king's in the case of an overlord). In exchange, he vows to give him advice and military support as well as financial aid. If he does not respect his promise, he becomes a traitor and his fief is taken back. At the time this was no joke!

Duke William pays tribute to Harold for his bravery during the battles in which he joined him. He gives him arms. Harold becomes his vassal.

Detail from the Bayeux Tapestry/11th century. With special authorization from the town of Bayeux.

Chapter 2

William, Duke of Normandy

It is not that easy to become a duke! As a young man, William is ready to reign over Normandy but he will have to assert his authority on the local lords...

Chase

In early 1047, William is 20 years old. He is ready to lead the duchy. But the Norman lords see things differently: they have decided to get rid of him! They are called "the rebelling barons".

William has been warned: he runs away from the castle where he was staying in Valognes, Manche. Chased by his enemies, he goes through a great part of what is now known as Calvados. He eventually finds refuge in Falaise, the town where he was born. Phew!

William, a Duke at last!

In the following months, William gets ready to fight against the Norman lords. He asks Henri 1st, King of France, for help. In the early summer of 1047 the two sides come face to face in Val-ès-Dunes near Caen. William wins the battle: this victory allows him to establish peace in Normandy. The bastard's authority is settled at last.

Franck Dion/Town of Falaise.

In the Middle Ages, the sword is the major weapon used by knights like William. The point is used to pierce, the edge to cut. The sword can also be used to knock out the enemy!

Eu Tourist Information Centre.

Surprise attack

A few years later, the duchy is threatened again by several lords like the Count of Anjou. William defends himself and even manages to extend his duchy. Thus, the power of Normandy is starting to worry the King of France, who sends out his soldiers. In 1057 William hides in a forest with his men and attacks his enemies by surprise. He wins another battle. In 1059 they make peace. But is this going to last?

Hurray for the newly-weds!

At the age of 23, William is not married yet. He chooses Matilda, grand-daughter of Robert the Pious and niece of King Henry 1st. Legend has it that she said no at first! But William has his mind set and eventually wins her heart. They get married in 1050 in Eu, Seine-Maritime.

Harald Mourreau/Hag'Dik.

William's knights wear a Norman helmet: it is a cone-shaped steel helmet. It has an oblong strip to protect the nose.

A huge castle

When King Henri 1st invades Normandy in 1057, William wishes there were a castle in Caen. The location is perfect to keep watch over the duchy and to protect it. He thus has a fortress built there around 1060. It is one of the biggest in France. During his reign, William also expands the Norman towns and has abbeys built. He shows great leadership!

The wall around the Caen castle was repaired several times as centuries went by. At the time of William, the top probably had crenels. All around it is the gap, not filled with water, which serves as a defence against the enemy.

Guichard/Caen Tourist Information Centre.

Antiquities Museum Y. Deslandes.

Who lived in the castles?

As soon as the castle is built, the lord decides who will be allowed to live in it. His family lives in a house or in the donjon if it is big enough. The kitchens, the stables, the forge and some cottages are used to accommodate the craftsmen and the lord's servants. A chapel is used to celebrate the important times in the life of a Christian society, like christenings. If they are under attack, the peasants of the village can also take refuge inside the walls. That could make quite a lot of people!

Learn+

Castles in the Middle Ages

Until the time of William, castles are mere wooden towers built on a mound of earth and surrounded by a fence. But little by little wood is replaced by stone. Stone castles are born!

From the 9th to the 11th centuries,
a castle is a simple square wooden tower built on a large mound of earth. Thus, it is more difficult to attack. It is surrounded by a farmyard, a fence and a ditch. It is called the Motte and Bailey castle. Some can still be seen in Normandy.

From the 11th to the 13th centuries,
the first wooden donjons appear. The fence is reinforced by square or round towers. It depends what you like the most!

From the 13th to the 14th centuries,
the donjon is not systematically included. But the castle is protected by a double or a triple wooden wall. To feel safer!

In the 15th century,
wooden fortresses are very resistant. And some castles look like real palaces!

Guichard/Caen Tourist Information Centre.

The building of the castle in Caen starts in 1060. But its donjon is only built around 1120 and the two round towers of the fence around 1210. That is nearly a hundred years later!

Guichard/Caen Tourist Information Centre.

Chapter 3

Conquering England!

When the King of England dies, Harold dons the crown instead of William. The Duke of Normandy does not see it that way! With the help of his army, he decides to fight against Harold at Hastings, in England.

William, future King of England

In England, King Edward is getting older and he has no children. As he spent part of his life in France, he knows William. He chooses him as his heir. He sends Harold, his brother-in-law, to tell him the news. But when Edward dies in 1064, Harold takes William's place on the throne of England. He pretends that the old king told him to just before he died. Is he telling the truth? We are still not sure of the answer! Very angry at what looks like a betrayal to him, William decides to invade England.

Heading for England!

For months, the Normans get ready to conquer England. On September 10th, 1066, 500 ships sail out with more than 7 000 men, 3 000 horses, weapons and food onboard. But a storm makes them stop in the north of France. They sail back three weeks later and land on English shores on September 29th, 1066.

Detail from the Bayeux Tapestry/11th century. With special authorization from the town of Bayeux.

William hastily has ships built in order to land in England and to attack the English with his army. Shipbuilding yards settle in the Norman forest along the coasts for six months.

The battle of Hastings

King Harold, who has just won a victory over the Norwegians in the north of England, learns that William and his troops have just landed in the south. He goes there. He plans on surprising the invaders, but William attacks first. He is a quick one! On October 14th, 1066, the Normans and the English fight in Hastings. Harold dies in the battle. William is the victor: he becomes King of England. He is then called "William the Conqueror".

Long live the King!

William is crowned King of England on Christmas day 1066. In order to control his new kingdom, William lists everything there: lands, men, cattle, buildings...

A sad piece of news

While William is in England, Matilda rules Normandy. But in 1083 she dies during a plague epidemic. William is very sad because he loved her passionately.

Harald Mourreau/Hag'Dik.

In Hastings, William's army is going up the Battle hill where Harold's army is waiting. The fight is bloody!

Goodbye William...

When William comes back to Normandy, King Philip of France has taken the Vexin which is partly Norman. William is sick but he engages on another battle in summer 1087 to take the Vexin back. During the fight, he feels faint, falls from his horse and gets hurt. A few days later William dies. As he wished, he is buried in the Abbaye-aux-Hommes in Caen.

You can admire the statue of William on his horse in Falaise. He is depicted in his battle dress at the battle of Hastings.

Town of Falaise.

Which weapons did the knights use in Hastings?

At the battle of Hastings, William's army is well equipped! First walk the bowmen with their bows and arrows. Then come the walking soldiers, armed with pikes and javelins. The cavalrymen bring up the rear. They ride steeds fitted out with reins, stirrups and a leather bridle. As for Harold's army, they only fight walking. The English soldiers carry axes and shields. With such weapons, the fights are bloody!

Learn+

The first comic strip in history

"The first comic strip in history", the Bayeux tapestry tells the story of the conquest of England in 58 "images" with texts. This embroidery is more than 70 metres long and 50 centimetres high. It is big! Here are a few extracts.

The first scene of the Bayeux tapestry represents King Edward in the company of Harold. The old king asks his brother-in-law to tell William he will be his heir.

First in line, William boards with his soldiers. England, here we come!

On October 14th, 1066, William's army confronts the English in the south of England, in Hastings. In this scene, the Latin text reads : "Here, Englishmen and Frenchmen died as they fought."

Test

What kind of k

1 To win a fight, you must first:
- A Think it over and get organised.
- B Rush into the battle blindly.
- C Try to make peace.

2 What is your main quality?
- A You are methodical.
- B You are very courageous.
- C You can talk someone into doing something.

3 Which animal is on your coat of arms?
- A A lion.
- B A wolf.
- C A dove.

4 In a fight, your lord is killed :
- A You replace him as the leader.
- B You carry on fighting.
- C You make peace with the other side.

5 What could your nickname be?
- A The Wise One.
- B The Brave One.
- C The Gentle One.

6 If you were not a knight, you would like to be:
- A The King or the Queen.
- B A castle builder.
- C The King's messenger.

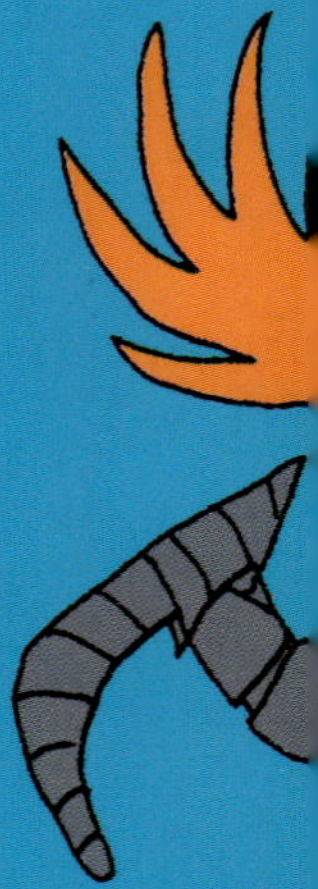

night would you be?

If you were a knight, would you be rather wise and peaceful, daring and reckless or else a fearsome army leader? Answer these questions and find out.

Answers to the test: For each question, circle the letter corresponding to your answer and then count how many A's, B's and C's you have got. Have a look page 24 to know who you are.

Quiz time
William the Conqueror

1 Where was William born?
A In Caen.
B In Falaise.
C In Hastings.

2 What was William's nickname when he was a kid?
A The Big Lie.
B The Black Bard.
C The Bastard.

3 What do you call a territory that a duke rules?
A A duchy.
B A domain.
C A county.

4 What is the name of William's wife?
A Matilda. B Gaëlle. C Nathalie.

5 How many children do William and Matilda have?
A 1 son and 1 daughter.
B 5 sons and 4 daughters.
C 4 sons and 5 daughters.

6 In 1066, William becomes King:
A Of Norway.
B Of England.
C Of France.

7 Who wants to take William's place on the throne of England?
A Harold. B Edward. C Philippe.

8 Where does the battle which enables William to become King of England take place?
A In Caen. B In London. C In Hastings.

9 What is William's nickname as an adult?
A The Conqueror.
B The Norman.
C The Bastard.

10 What is the object which you can see in Bayeux and which represents the conquest of England?
A A vase.
B A tapestry.
C A poster.

Solutions:
see page 24

This way, please!

In Seine-Maritime

Jumièges Abbey

Opened by William the Conqueror, this great abbey is a perfect testimony of architecture in the Middle Ages. In the summer it is lit up for romantic night walks!

Abbaye de Jumièges,
24 rue Guillaume-le-Conquérant.
Tel. 02 35 37 24 02. www.jumieges.fr

Jibédé.

Saint-Wandrille Abbey

This abbey was restored at the time of William. Visit the ruins of the former abbey-church and today's church.

Abbaye de Saint-Wandrille,
2 rue Saint-Jacques. Tel. 02 35 96 23 11.
www.st-wandrille.com

William-the-Conqueror Tour

This tour takes you to towns in Upper Normandy which are linked to William: Lillebonne, Fécamp, Dieppe...

The booklet is available on
www.seine-maritime-tourisme.com

In Calvados...

Falaise Castle

In the castle where William was born, discover what the Middle Ages were like! With an audio-guide, follow a journey through the donjons and visit the lord's house. Then discover the vegetable chapel built in the former farmyard of the castle.
Château Guillaume-le-Conquérant, place Guillaume-le-Conquérant. Tel. 02 31 41 61 44. www.chateau-guillaume-le-conquerant.fr

Guichard/Caen Tourist Information Centre.

Abbaye-aux-Hommes (Men's Abbey)

Founded in 1063 by William the Conqueror, the Abbaye-aux-Hommes now serves as Caen's City Council and William's grave is in the abbey-church. Discover them through fascinating guided tours!
Abbaye-aux-Hommes, Esplanade Jean-Marie Louvel. Tel. 02 31 30 42 81. www.ville-caen.fr

Caen Castle

Built in 1060 by William the Conqueror, this castle is one of the biggest fortresses in Europe. Also visit the archaeological remnants and the restored ramparts. You can then visit the museum of Normandy, located inside the castle. A bust of William is on display there.
Tel. 02 31 27 14 14. www.chateau.caen.fr Musée de Normandie. Tel. 02 31 30 47 60. www.musee-de-normandie.caen.fr

Abbaye-aux-Dames (Women's Abbey)

Founded by Matilda, William's wife, this abbey is now the headquarters of Lower Normandy's Conseil Régional. Guided tours help you discover this magnificient 11th century building, built with the famous Caen Stone.
Abbaye-aux-Dames, Place Reine Mathilde. Tel. 02 31 06 98 98. www.cr-basse-normandie.fr

Notre-Dame Cathedral

Built in the 11th century, this Romanesque-style cathedral was opened in the presence of William the Conqueror. With a guided tour, discover the chapter and the treasure room!

Cathédrale Notre-Dame, in Bayeux.
Tel. 02 31 92 14 21.

Bayeux Tapestry

This gigantic 70-meters long, 50-centimeters high embroidered tapestry is the first « comic strip » in history! It tells the story of the conquest of England by William in 1066. It is a unique document listed as world heritage by UNESCO.

Musée de la Tapisserie de Bayeux, centre Guillaume-le-Conquérant.
Tel. 02 31 51 25 50.
www.tapisserie-bayeux.fr

"The Fabulous Epic" tour

A tour with signs along the way takes you through Calvados on William the Conqueror's trail. You will see five major spots and ten minor ones. At each stop, your booklet sets activities for you to do. Become unbeatable on William the Conqueror's story!

Comité départemental du tourisme. Tel. 02 31 27 90 30. www.calvados-tourisme.com

...and also out of Normandy

Harald Mourreau/Hag'Dik.

Hastings Castle

After the battle, William had a massive castle built in Hastings. Part of it was destroyed but you can visit the remnants! A multimedia presentation tells the story of the famous battle and the castle. King Harold and William are parts in this presentation! Then you can go and see the haunted donjons!

Hastings Castle, England. Tel. +44 (0)1424 44 44 12.
http://new.discoverhastings.co.uk/castle/castle.shtml

Dictionary

Pilgrimage : journey to a holy place, here Jerusalem.

Duchy : territory under the authority of a duke.

Steed: horse used in fights in the Middle Ages

Test scores

You have got mostly A's: You would not be a simple knight: you would be an army leader! You take time to think and to work out a plan before you go to fight. You like taking initiatives, you are authoritative and you know how to earn respect. But do not forget to take the others' opinions into account!

You have got mostly B's: You would be a reckless knight. You like action and if fighting is required, you rush into it! You are full of energy and you are not afraid of anything. Those on your side know they can rely on you. But do not be stubborn: knights are always stronger when they are together!

You have got mostly C's: You would be a peaceful knight. As far as you are concerned, to fight and kill your enemies is not a solution. You believe that dialogue is a better way to settle differences than weapons. This is very reasonable. But do not let others tread on your toes, though. Assert yourself with words!

Quiz answers

1B ; 2C ; 3A ; 4A ; 5C ; 6B ; 7A ; 8C ; 9A ; 10B.

Discover all our books on www.normandie-junior.com

Did you enjoy this book? You will also like Normandie Junior magazine! Published quarterly, it enables you to discover what is new and what is treasured in Normandy. Lively reports, enthralling files, games, tests, comics and a mini-novel... Hours of reading and fascinating activities! Normandie Junior is the favourite magazine of 7 to 12 year-old Normans!

Normandie junior
Le magazine régional des 7-12 ans

On sale at newsstands and on subscription.
Normandie Junior: 47, place du Général-de-Gaulle – 76000 Rouen – Tel. 02 32 10 60 64. www.normandie-junior.com